THE
REALLY
GOOD GAME
BOOK

The
REALLY
GOOD
GAME
BOOK

CHARLES TONGUE

ROBSON BOOKS

First published in Great Britain in 1988 by Robson Books Ltd,
Bolsover House, 5-6 Clipstone Street, London W1P 7EB.

Copyright © Charles Tongue 1988
Book designed by the Design Shop, Reigate.

Tongue, Charles
    Really Good Game Book
    1. Party games – Collections
    I. Title
    793.2

    ISBN 0 86051 556 7

Printed by A. Wheaton & Co Ltd, Exeter, Devon.
Bound by Dorstel Press Ltd, Harlow, Essex.

CONTENTS

INDOOR
◆ ENERGETIC
◆ GAMES

Spoons

RULES

Players gather in a large circle on the floor, and each receives six playing cards. In the middle of the circle is a pile of spoons, one fewer than the number of players.

The cards are turned up one by one around the circle and when a consecutive pair is revealed all players dive for the spoons. Whoever emerges without a spoon is the loser. If you want to be less violent you can substitute fully-inflated balloons for the spoons.

HOW TO WIN

The game can be played as a knock-out, with a decreasing number of spoons or with a forfeit for the loser in each round.

RISKS

Limited injury to body and spoons. Risks can be increased by placing the spoons in another room, house or street!

WHAT YOU NEED

Playing cards, spoons or balloons and at least six players.

FALLOUT

RULES

Two teams each stand in a tight circle and a feather is dropped in the middle of each circle from above. Each team must prevent the feather falling to the ground while avoiding physical contact with it. Any form of upward draught is acceptable.

This game becomes more demanding if the two teams are mixed up together and the feathers are dropped only about three feet apart.

WHAT YOU NEED

Two feathers and at least six players.

FORFEIT

1

Sing two verses of any Beatles song.

PYRAMIDS

RULES

This one could be useful training for architecture students. Split into two teams. Each team writes down a list of parts of the body equal to the number of people in the team. The lists are then exchanged, and each team must arrange itself into a shape involving all its members such that only the items on the list are in contact with the floor.

It is helpful before beginning to play the game to agree certain parts of the body which must not be included and also to set a time limit of, say, three minutes!

HOW TO WIN

It's too easy just to write down a nose, an ear and an elbow, so to beat the other team you have got to set them a task which they cannot achieve and then prove it's possible by doing it with your own team.

RISKS

Extensive destruction of fixtures and fittings.
Bruised and broken limbs.

WHAT YOU NEED

Pencils, paper and at least six players.

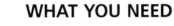

FORFEIT

2

Do an impersonation of anybody in the room. The others must then guess who you were impersonating.

GET KNOTTED

RULES

One player is excluded, the rest stand in a circle and link hands. They then twine themselves into a tight knot by stepping over arms, through legs, etc. while still holding hands.

When the bodies are thoroughly entwined, the excluded player must physically untie the knot while the hands remain linked.

HOW TO WIN

It's best to play this game against the clock, allowing the outsider five minutes to get everyone unscrambled.

ANOTHER KNOTING

RULES

Another way to start this game is to get everyone to stand in a circle facing inwards with their eyes closed, and their arms outstretched in front of them. They must then hold any hand that their hand comes into contact with and again the outsider has the task of unravelling the knot of arms while the hands remain linked.

RISKS

Intimate overheating.

WHAT YOU NEED

At least four players.

FORFEIT

3

Imitate a crocodile swimming across a crowded estuary.

Are you there Moriarty?

RULES

Two players are blindfolded and arm themselves with rolled newspapers. They then lie face down on the floor opposite each other, heads about one foot apart, and grip each other's left forearm.

The object is to hit the opponent's head with your newspaper. To find where it is, you take turns to demand: 'Are you there, Moriarty?', to which the opponent must make an audible reply. You are only allowed one hit for each 'Moriarty'.

HOW TO WIN

This game is essentially for the benefit of the audience, so you can win by proving your bravery and fortitude under physical threat, or more simply by three direct hits on your opponent's cranium.

RISKS

Injuries to head and face. Occasional brain damage (this game is a favourite at superpower summit meetings).

WHAT YOU NEED

Two blindfolds and two newspapers.

FORFEIT

4

Tell jokes until someone laughs.

FORFEIT

5

Drink alcohol from the belly-button of the player on your left.

BLIND MAN'S
Custard

RULES

For this game you split into two teams and elect two
champions in each team. The champions sit opposite
each other at a table and are blindfolded. They are
then each presented with a small bowl of custard and
a spoon and each must feed the custard to their
partner as quickly as possible. The rest of the team
can help by giving directions to their champions.

HOW TO WIN

The team achieving the fastest combined feed time is
the winner. Strict rules regarding spoon accuracy
and allowable wastage must be agreed beforehand.

RISKS

Custard-related mess.
Custard-related nausea.

WHAT YOU NEED

Custard or similar food, blindfolds, spoons and at
least six players.

INDOOR FOOTBALL

RULES

Each player ties an inflated balloon on a short piece of string to their ankle. When the game begins each player must stamp out the other players' balloons while maintaining their own intact. Players must withdraw as soon as their balloons are burst, and semi-inflated balloons are not allowed.

HOW TO WIN

The last person with an intact balloon is the winner.

WHAT YOU NEED

Balloons, length of string, and at least six players.

BOTTLE *of* SMOKE

RULES

The players get into two teams and each person writes down the title of a book, film, play or song. These titles are put into a hat and given to the opposing team. Then the team members take turns to create a living sculpture to depict the title they have drawn from the hat.

As models for this sculpture, they use members of the other team, and purely from the visual information of the sculpture, without any verbal prompting, their own team must guess the title.

Charades conventions can be used at the outset to indicate whether it is a film, book, etc. but otherwise this sculpture must speak for itself.

HOW TO WIN

Team-guessing should be done against the clock, with three, two and one points allocated respectively for guesses within one, two or three minutes.

WHAT YOU NEED

Pencils and paper and at least eight players.

FORFEIT
6

Swap all your clothes with the nearest member of the opposite sex.

FORFEIT 7

Blindfold one of the other players and give them a box of matches. Then give them the exact instructions needed to open the box and light one of the matches. The blindfolded player must only act on instruction.

CHINLESS WONDER

RULES

Here are the best of the ancient team relay games. They seem to suffer from their close association with the Fifties, but you can sharpen them up by playing them simultaneously or maybe surreptitiously during a heavy meeting.

The essentials of all these relays are two teams standing in a line and passing, without the assistance of their hands, various items down the line from one end to the other. The usual items are oranges under the chin, Polo mints on straws, and a key on a piece of string inside everyone's clothing. The correct degree of confusion can be generated if all three are moving up and down the lines at the same time and preferably in opposite directions.

HOW TO WIN

Speed is the key issue.

WHAT YOU NEED

Polo mints, straws, oranges, two lengths of string, two keys and at least eight players.

SUCK & BLOW

RULES

This is a good new addition to the relay format, involving a playing card passing from mouth to mouth down the line. The usual rules of no hand contact apply, and the card must not be held between the lips, but must be retained on the mouth by sucking. When it's time to transfer it to the next player the sucker begins to blow and the next player begins to suck.

WHAT YOU NEED

Two playing cards and at least eight players.

MURDER
IN THE DARK

RULES

If you've got good detectives, the interrogation should be as funny as wandering around in the dark.

To play this, a detective and murderer are chosen by dealing playing cards, matches, etc.

The method of murder (usually two taps on the head or shoulder) is agreed, and the detective withdraws to the 'station'.

All lights are then extinguished and everyone meanders around the house for some time while the murderer stalks the prey. When the murder is committed, the victim waits around three seconds (to give the murderer a chance to escape) then collapses with a horrible scream.

The detective dashes to the scene and takes on the interrogation of all the suspects to find out what exactly has happened.

During this interrogation only the murderer is allowed to lie and after summing up the evidence the detective must guess who committed the crime.

THE TRIAL

When the detective has guessed the killer, everyone else votes Yes or No to the choice. If the detective is wrong he/she must do a forfeit unless the majority agreed with the choice. In that case the person chosen must do the forfeit. If the detective chose right, the murderer does the forfeit.

HOW TO WIN

Guess the murderer.

RISKS

Unbecoming behaviour in the dark.

WHAT YOU NEED

Playing cards, complete darkness, a number of rooms and at least six players.

INSIDE OUT

RULES

This is another game for pairs. One member of each pair puts on his shirt, jacket and overcoat inside out and in reverse order, so that the shirt is on the outside. The player then links hands with his partner and attempts to exchange the clothes so that they finish up on the other body in the correct order and right side out.

HOW TO WIN

The fastest pair to exchange clothes are the winners; the pairs can compete simultaneously or individually against the clock while the rest watch.

RISKS

Carpet-burns on the elbows and shoulders.

WHAT YOU NEED

Two sets of shirts, jackets, overcoats, and at least six players.

ADAPTATION

More advanced players may prefer this game to include trousers and underpants, and blindfolds.

GOODWOOD
RACES

RULES

This is a game for a large group organized into pairs. The men get down on their hands and knees like horses facing into the middle of a circle. They then play snap and the women meander around the back of the circle keeping constantly on the move. When one of the men yells snap, the women must rush to their partner and climb on to his back.

HOW TO WIN

The last person on to a man can either be out, and the numbers diminish until the winner is found, or a forfeit can be imposed and the game begun again with the same numbers.

CATERPILLA

RULES

The first thing is to agree a race-track which is at least twelve feet wide and ten feet long. You need two teams, each lying straight out on the floor and closely packed together, with the front end of each team lying along the start line.

The two teams then race along the course, their means of progression being for the player at the back of the line to roll over all the others to the front. This should be done in a continuous rhythm, but arms cannot be used and should be kept rigidly at the sides at all times.

HOW TO WIN

The first 'caterpillar' fully to cross the finish line is the winner.

RISKS

This may not be a good idea after a large meal.

WHAT YOU NEED

At least eight players.

NUTTERS

RULES

Two players each fold arms and stand on one leg. They then attempt to knock each other off balance by hopping into each other at speed.

HOW TO WIN

As soon as any player touches the floor with both feet they are out. This game should be played as a knock-out to find the ultimate nutter who may then be ordered to do at least three forfeits.

INDOOR

♦

INTIMATE

♦

GAMES

BODY SEARCH

RULES

Here's a game that could have come from the Police Training Manual. Two players are blindfolded and a safety pin is 'planted' somewhere on their clothing. The rest of the players watch. The two then stand opposite each other and try to feel their way to the other's safety pin before their own is found.

HOW TO WIN

This game can be played as a knock-out. In each round the first to find the pin is the winner.

WHAT YOU NEED

Two blindfolds, two safety-pins and at least six players.

RISKS

Depends where you put the pin!

GAME 18

gummies

RULES

In this elaborate excuse for extended kissing, two players are identified as outsiders. The lights are dimmed and the rest of the players form into couples and kiss. When their lips part the outsiders who are roaming around observing can dive between a couple and beginning kissing whichever of the two they prefer. That leaves a new outsider to roam until they can break into someone else's clinch, but this can only happen when the two pairs of lips are parted.

HOW TO WIN

Depending on the company, you may win by being an outsider all the time or by avoiding ever being an outsider. Maybe it's one way to stay off the alcohol!

33

Vampire

RULES

First you have to choose a vampire by drawing cards or matches. Then you turn the lights off and everyone meanders around the house. There must be absolute darkness, and the vampire prowls among the players stalking a victim.

The vampire attacks by way of a delicate bite on the neck after which the victim also becomes a vampire and must go in search of new victims.

HOW TO WIN

Avoid falling victim to a vampire.

FORFEIT
8

Go from one corner of the room to the opposite corner without touching the floor.

Therapy

ADAPTATIONS

You can extend the game by introducing the rule that if a vampire bites another vampire they both revert to normality.

Alternatively, you can instruct all players to go down on all fours, change the mode of attack to a bite on the buttock, and call the game Zombies.

FORFEIT

9

Be outlandishly theatrical in your movements for five minutes.

COMMUTERS

RULES

This game is really called Sardines, but it's quite like commuting. One player is elected to go off in the dark and hide themselves somewhere, preferably in a confined space in the house. The others wait a minute then follow to find the 'Sardine'. When they succeed they must squeeze in with the Sardine wherever he or she has chosen to hide.

The game continues until only one person remains wandering who has not yet found the Sardine. This person is the loser and must do a forfeit.

HOW TO WIN

Get to the Sardine first.

RISKS

The Sardine is most at risk from suffocation.

WHAT YOU NEED

At least eight players.

Travolta

RULES

This is a knock-out for large groups of people, and you need somewhere to dance and some music.

First you choose a leader and that person is blindfolded. The music goes on and everybody dances around in couples. At intervals the leader cuts the music and the couples must quickly adopt one of three possible positions. The positions are: 'Fireman's Lift' – one over the other's shoulder, 'Ventriloquist's Dummy' – one on the other's knee with hand up the back, and 'Hot Dog' – both lying on the floor one on top of the other.

Each time the music is cut, the leader allows a few seconds for the poses to be adopted, and then calls out one of them. All players who have adopted that pose are then eliminated.

HOW TO WIN

The last couple on the dance floor is the winner.

PASS THE
BANANA

RULES

Two teams stand in line, level with each other. The player at the front of each line places a banana between his or her thighs. The banana must be passed on down the line from thigh to thigh. There must be no hand contact with the banana at any stage. At the end of the line you need a suitable receptacle like a bucket for the banana to be flopped into.

HOW TO WIN

The first team to get their banana in the receptacle is the winner.

RISKS

This game can be hard on bananas, so they should be firm at the outset.

WHAT YOU NEED

Bananas and at least six players.

ON THE BOTTLE

RULES

Here is a practical joke game.

Get two players, opposite sex but not 'partners', and screen them off in some way from the rest of the party, so that they can be heard but not seen.

The two players must lay a wine bottle flat on the floor and then both balance on it together for ten seconds. Explain that everyone else will be listening and timing them to see how quick they are. The fun comes for the rest of the party to whom you have explained that you have instructed the two players to re-enact their first sexual experience.

WHAT YOU NEED

Wine bottle and screen, or adjacent room.

Cyril smith

RULES

The players divide up according to sex, and one of the two groups is blindfolded and sits down in a row.

The idea of the game is to identify the other team members by certain parts of their bodies, so at the beginning the parts of the body which will be used (ankle, knee, stomach, etc.) must be agreed upon.

The blindfolded team hold out their hands and each member of the other team must walk down the line presenting the selected part of the body for ten seconds to each hand. Then the blindfolded team discuss who it was, and call out their group conclusion. When every member of the team has been inspected, the roles are reversed.

HOW TO WIN

The team with the highest number of correct guesses is the winner.

HO HO HO!

RULES

This is a group sharing experience scenario game. Everyone lies down in a ring with their heads on the stomach of the next person in the circle. The lead player goes 'Ho-Ho' from the pit of the stomach, and this automatically jars the head of the next player round the circle. It is then their turn to go 'Ho-Ho-Ho' and so on around the circle with one more 'Ho' for each consecutive player.

It's supposed to make you laugh!

FORFEIT

10

Do a head-stand against the wall and balance a cup on your foot for thirty seconds.

Noah's Ark
IN THE DARK

RULES

Before the game begins, you need to mark cards with the names of animals, two cards for each type of animal, and ensure there are the same number of cards as players. You can split the cards into two batches, and the players into sexes.

Each player picks a card and the lights are extinguished. The players then take on the character of the animal on their card and they must find their partner by calling with the relevant animal sound.

It's best to avoid obvious creatures like dogs and cats, and worms might be a problem too!

HOW TO WIN

This is a race to find partners so the last animals still calling are the losers and must perform a forfeit.

WHAT YOU NEED

Card, pen, several completely dark rooms and at least ten people.

IN
bed

RULES

This is a public practical joke so you must tell everyone except the victim what's happening. The victim is told to lie on the floor and that this guessing game is a kind of test of their imagination. They're completely covered with a blanket on the floor, and it is then explained to them that there is one specific item of their clothing which they have to give you to pass the test. They must guess what the item is and pass it out to you.

So they begin passing out shoes and jackets and socks, and all the spectators continue to assure them that they haven't guessed the correct item until they are finally undressed, and they still haven't passed the test.

At last they realize it's the blanket – but is it too late to hand it over?

INDOOR CALM GAMES

TRACK RECORD

RULES

Within two teams each player thinks of three strange, amusing or unlikely things that have happened to them in the past. These must be true.

These short anecdotes are written down anonymously and passed in a hat to the opposing team. The teams then take turns to read out an anecdote and guess which member of the other team it applies to.

HOW TO WIN

Points are awarded for each correct guess, so the highest score wins.

WHAT YOU NEED

Pens and paper and at least six players.

SOY CATCHER

RULES

For this game the players arrange themselves in groups of three. One group leaves the room while the rest write down a sentence such as: 'The Hungarian swallow flies north after an icy winter'. This sentence is then passed to the group outside, only one of whom may read it.

Meanwhile the rest of the players are composing a set of 40 words which they will use to interrogate each of the three players outside to help them guess which of the three read the message.

So the interrogations take place. Each subject is told that they must provide word associations for the 40 words. The interrogators fire the 40 trigger words and watch out for distorted responses to the words that have been inserted which relate to the message, e.g. Swallow, Hungary, winter etc.

After each round the interrogators decide which of the three is the spy, and the spotlight passes on to the next team.

HOW TO WIN

Avoid detection.

WHAT YOU NEED

Pencil and paper.

CHARADES

RULES

This game can be played in teams against the clock or individually. Each player writes down the title of a song, film, play or book and these are either presented to the opposing team or placed in a hat.

Each person then takes a title and must communicate it to his or her own team without using any sounds. A time limit of three minutes can be imposed and higher points awarded if the mime is guessed within the first minute.

Playing without teams, the actor mimes to the whole group and the person who guesses the title takes the next turn.

HOW TO WIN

The team with the highest score wins.

WHAT YOU NEED

Pencils and paper and at least six players.

ADAPTATION

The game of charades is well known and good fun, and there are now a number of adaptations to add variety.

The same basic idea can be used in the context of drawings instead of miming. This is best using two teams playing simultaneously, one player from each team trying to communicate a film, book, play or song to team members by drawing the clues.

chinese CHARADES

RULES

This requires two teams, one acting and the other spectating. All the acting team leave the room except one, who is given the charade by the spectating team.

One member of the acting team comes into the room and the team leader who is already there has 30 seconds to act out the charade. Then the third team member comes in and player No. 2 has to act it to player No. 3 again in 30 seconds. This continues down the line until the last member of the team comes in and after 30 seconds they must tell the spectating team what the charade was.

Botticelli

RULES

One player, Sarah, thinks of a famous person and tells everyone the first letter of their name, e.g., S. The others think of people whose names start with the same first letter. They ask, e.g. 'Are you a famous racing driver?' Sarah must think of someone who fits the description and says, 'No, I'm not Ayrton Senna.' This is O.K. even if the questioner was thinking of, say, Jackie Stewart. If Sarah can't think of anyone who fits the description she must allow a direct question about the identity of her chosen person, i.e. 'Are you alive?' 'Are you male?' etc.

The game continues until the identity of the mystery person has been discovered.

HOW TO WIN

Guess the identity of Sarah's person.

WHAT YOU NEED

A minimum of two players, but four or more would be much better.

SIMPLIFICATION

The game can be shortened by adapting the rules. If Sarah can't think of a famous racing driver beginning with S, she must say the next letter of the name.

FATAL
attraction

RULES

This game needs good interrogators and good liars. Two of each are chosen, and the suspects are told they must account for their movements, say, between 7 and 8 pm last Wednesday evening, when they are thought to have been in bed together. Their story must cover them both, so they leave the room to decide on their alibi. They are then called in individually to be cross-examined by the interrogator. After both have been interrogated the other players who have been spectating must decide whether the alibi has held up or not.

FORFEIT
11

Explain the significance of Eastern religion to a modern Western capitalist society in thirty seconds.

Donald
DUCK

RULES

All the players sit in a circle. Each writes the name of a famous person on a piece of paper and sticks it (without showing it to them) on the forehead of the player to their left. So each player can see everybody else's names on the foreheads but they can't see their own.

Each player then takes turns to ask the group Yes/No questions to find out the name that is written on their own forehead. When the answer to a question is 'Yes', that player may ask another; when the answer is 'No' the turn passes to the left.

HOW TO WIN

The first three players to guess correctly who they are are the winners.

WHAT YOU NEED

Pens and paper, sellotape or Rizlas, and at least four players.

WORDS
to say

RULES

This is a game for dinner parties. When the guests arrive you give each one a card with an obscure word on it. All the cards are different. When the guests are sitting down at the table they must make someone say the word on their card. The first to succeed is the winner, and must do two forfeits.

WHAT YOU NEED

Cards with obscure words written on them.

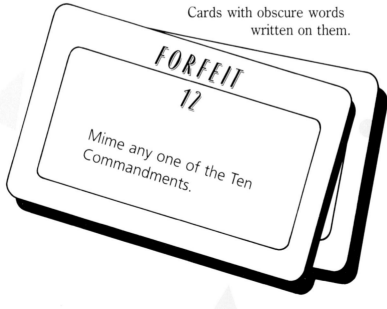

FORFEIT

12

Mime any one of the Ten Commandments.

THE D'CTIONARY GAME

RULES

Two teams take turns to choose extremely obscure words from the dictionary.

Having chosen a word, each member of the team presents a definition of its meaning. Among these plausible definitions is the correct one and all the others are false.

When all definitions have been heard, the other team vote for the one they believe to be true.

HOW TO WIN

After a series of rounds, the team with the most correct guesses wins.

WHAT YOU NEED

A large dictionary and at least six players.

ADVERB DINNER

RULES

This game can be played as a back-drop to other activities, so it is ideal to run during a dinner party. When the guests arrive each is given a card on which is written an adverb. All the adverbs are different, and the object is for each guest to act during the first thirty minutes of the meal after the fashion of the adverb.

After that time everyone reverts to their normal behaviour and the players must guess what each other's adverbs were.

WHAT YOU NEED

Cards with adverbs written on them.

HOW TO WIN

If no one remotely guesses your adverb you must do a forfeit.

chinese ROULETTE

RULES

One player leaves the room while the others select someone from the group whose personality they must all take on.

On returning, the excluded player must guess who has been chosen by asking oblique questions such as: 'What sort of tree [or car, or animal, or country, etc.] would I be if I were the person you've chosen?"

The excluded player may only ask one question of each member of the group, and then must guess whom they were all describing.

HOW TO WIN

Guess correctly.

WHAT YOU NEED

At least five players who know each other fairly well.

MAXWELL

RULES

One person, e.g. Robert, leaves the room while the rest each write down an amusing or perceptive observation about him. The group then choose the best three statements and invite Robert back in.

The three statements are read out, and Robert must decide who made each. One point is awarded for each correct guess.

WHAT YOU NEED

Pens and paper and at least six players who all know each other fairly well.

FORFEIT

13

Make lewd suggestions to any member of the opposite sex for fifteen seconds without laughing.

WAVING and DROWNING

RULES

One player leaves the room while the others select adverbs which must then govern all their behaviour.

The outsider returns and tries to guess the adverb by getting each of the group to perform specific tasks, such as taking off a shoe or opening a bottle, in the manner of the adverb.

HOW TO WIN

The outsider has two chances to guess the adverb and then has the right to nominate the next outsider.

WHAT YOU NEED

At least five players.

Daydream BELIEVERS

RULES

The players get into two teams, and each writes down his or her own fantasy under various chosen headings. These fantasies can be best or worst, and the categories should be such things as murdering an enemy, relationship with another person, sex, etc.

The fantasies are written anonymously and presented in a hat to the opposing team.

Each team then takes turns to read out a fantasy and decide who in the opposing team it belongs to.

HOW TO WIN

When all the fantasies have been read and the authors guessed, the truth can be revealed, and the team with the most correct guesses is the winner.

WHAT YOU NEED

Pens and paper and at least six players.

IN THE PUB

FIZZ BU

RULES – 1

Players sit in a circle and take turns to count aloud from one. In place of any multiple of five the player concerned must substitute the word 'fizz' and for multiples of seven must substitute the word 'buzz'.

RULES – 2

This is a word association game played to a clapping rhythm. Players sit in a circle all clapping a beat: Clap, Clap, Gap, Clap, Clap, Gap, etc. The gap passes from player to player around the circle and must be filled in sequence around the circle with a word associated with the previous player's word.

HOW TO WIN

If you miss a 'fizz' or 'buzz', or can't think of a word before the next clap, you're out. Last one in wins and the first three out must do a forfeit.

CLAP

WHAT YOU NEED

At least four players

DEVELOPMENT

Both games must be played as fast as possible, and for the experienced players can run simultaneously in opposite directions around the circle.

FORFEIT
14

Limbo dance under an obstacle which is three feet off the ground.

DIRTY WINKER

RULES

Choose a murderer by drawing matches.

It's important that everyone sits in a circle so they can clearly see each other's faces. The murderer must try to kill each of the other players by winking at them. The wink must be seen by the victim who allows ten seconds before 'dying'.

All the others try to identify the murderer without being killed and if they see a wink take place which is not aimed at them they can accuse the murderer. If their accusation is wrong, they are automatically eliminated.

HOW TO WIN

Kill everyone.

WHAT YOU NEED

Matches and at least five players.

Limericks

RULES

Players get into two teams. Each team takes turns to give the opponents the first two lines of a limerick. The other team must provide the next three lines to finish the verse.

Alternatively this can be played around a circle with each person adding a line.

HOW TO WIN

Apart from literary style and humour, the objective must be speed, so anyone failing to provide the required line within 30 seconds must do a forfeit.

FORFEIT
15

Pick up a matchbox with your bare foot and raise it to your mouth.

JAM
ROLY POLY

RULES

This game is based on the old Oscar Wilde trick of describing people in completely outlandish and irrelevant ways, and then amazing listeners by a convoluted explanation of why the description is justified.

So the rules are that one person thinks of a thing – anything, and the others, not knowing what it is, take turns to suggest what the item is like. They could say, 'Your thought is like a teapot', or 'Your thought is like a tomato'.

When each of the players has suggested an analogy the first declares what the thing actually is and the others must quickly explain what is the connection between their own suggestion and the nominated item.

In this example the item turns out to be a book, so the explanation would be a teapot is like a book because it has some leaves, and a tomato is like a book because it is sometimes read/red.

HOW TO WIN

This game must be played quickly, so each player can be allowed only 30 seconds to come up with an explanation. Anyone who completely fails must do a forfeit.

ADAPTATION

For really creative people the next step is to explain why the chosen analogy cannot be correct.

FORFEIT

16

Compose a lusty rhyme for a Christmas card.

Cake Cream Custard

RULES

Players sit in a circle and choose a letter of the alphabet and a category, e.g., food, pop groups, or songs.

They then take turns around the circle to name something that corresponds to the letter and category that has been chosen. This game must be played fast and no repetition is allowed.

HOW TO WIN

Failure to nominate results in elimination or a forfeit. The winner is the last person still adding new items within the category.

COMPLICATION

When naming songs, you can stipulate that the next player around the circle must sing the first line of the nominated song before they can make their own choice.

WHAT YOU NEED

At least six players.

Wordsworth

RULES

One player, Theresa, is nominated, and she is given a letter of the alphabet. In the following one minute she must list all the nouns she can think of beginning with that letter. She then nominates the next player and letter, and so on until all players have had a turn. Agreement must be reached beforehand on which letters are impossible.

HOW TO WIN

Someone must keep a score of the words listed and the top scorer wins, and must do a forfeit.

WHAT YOU NEED

At least three players.

FORFEIT
17

Eat a dry Weetabix in
thirty seconds.

MARK *of* CAIN

RULES

Sitting in a circle the players each adopt a different biblical name. They then take turns around the circle to recite 'I, Rebecca, have no spots, how many spots has thou, Elija?' addressing the player on their left by their adopted name.

This sequence continues around the circle until a player either forgets their own or the next player's name. They are then dotted on the forehead with a red pen or lipstick. Each time an error is made a further red spot is added and the players must remember how many spots they have when the announce, 'I, Rebecca, have . . . spots . . . '

If two round, are completed without error the names are shifted one place to the right around the circle.

HOW TO WIN

When one player has five spots the game ends and the player with the fewest spots is the winner. The player with five spots must do forfeits.

FORFEIT

19

Impersonate a hedgehog crossing the M25.

FORFEIT

18

Hum the theme tune from any non-current television programme.

Chancellor's

BOX

RULES

All players hold three coins behind their backs. They then bring out any number from zero to three in a closed fist.

Each player then has a turn to guess the total number of coins in the fists. No two players may make the same guess.

HOW TO WIN

If you guess the correct number of coins you win; if you want to use this as a gambling game the coins must all be of the same value, and the winner takes the lot. If no one guesses correctly the round can be repeated, or those coins can be put aside as the kitty which goes to the next winner.

BIG BAND

RULES

With everyone sitting in a circle, a group leader is elected. The rest of the group nominate a tune and begin playing imaginary instruments to the tune. The leader begins playing one of the instruments that have been chosen.

The leader can then change instruments, say from trumpet to guitar, and all guitar players must respond by swapping to the trumpet. Anyone who misses their cue to change instruments is out, and the leader continues to change until only one other instrument remains.

HOW TO WIN

The last remaining instrument is the winner, and the first two players to be eliminated must do forfeits.

THE ID

RULES

Here are two games which involve passing items around a circle in a specific way to conform with a code. To break the code you need inspirational thought which some people just don't have.

Idiot I: Pass a pair of scissors around the circle, saying 'I pass these scissors to you crossed' – or 'I pass these scissors to you uncrossed'. As the scissors pass from person to person you as leader must decree whether the pass is valid or not. Eventually most people will realize that the crossing or uncrossing of the scissors refers to whether the passer's legs are crossed or not.

Idiot II: The same rules apply to the Holiday Game; you say, 'I'm going on holiday and I'm taking a towel', each player says, 'I'm coming and I'm bringing . . . ' whereupon you tell them whether they can come or not.

The key is that the thing they bring must begin with the first letter of the Christian name of the person on their left.

O T

HOW TO WIN

If they haven't got the code within five minutes, most people will never get it. The first two to catch on to the code must do excruciating forfeits for being so smug!

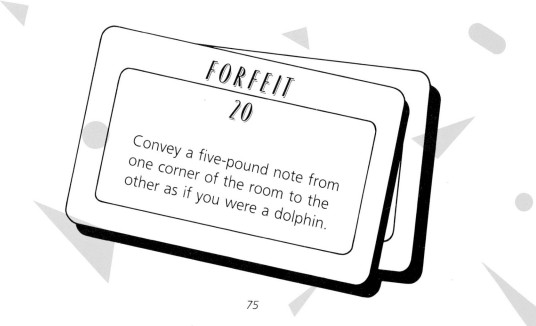

> ### FORFEIT
> ### 20
>
> Convey a five-pound note from one corner of the room to the other as if you were a dolphin.

OUTSIDE GAMES

CHUC

RULES

Players line up in pairs opposite each other with a water-filled balloon for each pair.

The players begin about three feet apart and throw the balloon across the gap to their partner. After each throw the partners move one pace further apart.

HOW TO WIN

The pair with the last intact balloon is the winner.

WHAT YOU NEED

Water, balloons and at least six players.

K. U. P.

FORFEIT
21

Do five press-ups while gripping a wine glass in your teeth and drinking the contents.

FORFEIT
22

Draw a flower, chosen by the rest of the group, on your own forehead.

FORFEIT
23

Hum the theme tune from any current radio programme.

Robber's DOG

RULES

This formula has developed as the basis of many weekend adventure games. One version is 'Kick the Dog'. The 'dog' (usually a tin can) is placed in the middle of a large area of land and one player is nominated to defend it, while the others all spread out and hide. Their objective is to get back and kick the 'dog', but if the defender spots them and calls their name before they touch the 'dog' they must retreat out of sight and try again. If the defender touches one of the players they also become defenders. When the 'dog' is kicked, a new defender is chosen.

HOME AND

RULES

Two teams each have their own 'dogs' to protect which represent their base camp. The object is to capture the opponent's 'dog' and get it back to your base. There must be a clear division midway between the two base camps showing each team's home territory.

If any player is touched outside their home territory they must withdraw to inside their territory before making another attack on the opponents' base. If a player succeeds in capturing the 'dog' they can only be stopped by two defenders touching them at the same time, in which case they must give up the 'dog' and return to home territory.

WHAT YOU NEED

For both these games you need large open areas of land with a mixture of open ground and cover.

AWAY

P A S S   T H

RULES

Two large teams each form a double row, cross arms and link hands with their team-mate opposite.

One team member stands alone at the end of the line and by lowering the structure of arms this person is lifted aboard. The object is to pass this 'flyer' along the line of arms without unlinking the hands. This is done by using an undulating wave motion and you must ensure that the 'flyer's' body remains rigid. At the end of the line the body is deposited on the ground beyond the agreed finish line.

HOW TO WIN

This game should be played as a race with two teams competing so the first 'flyer' over the finish line is the winner.

WHAT YOU NEED

At least eighteen people.

PERSON

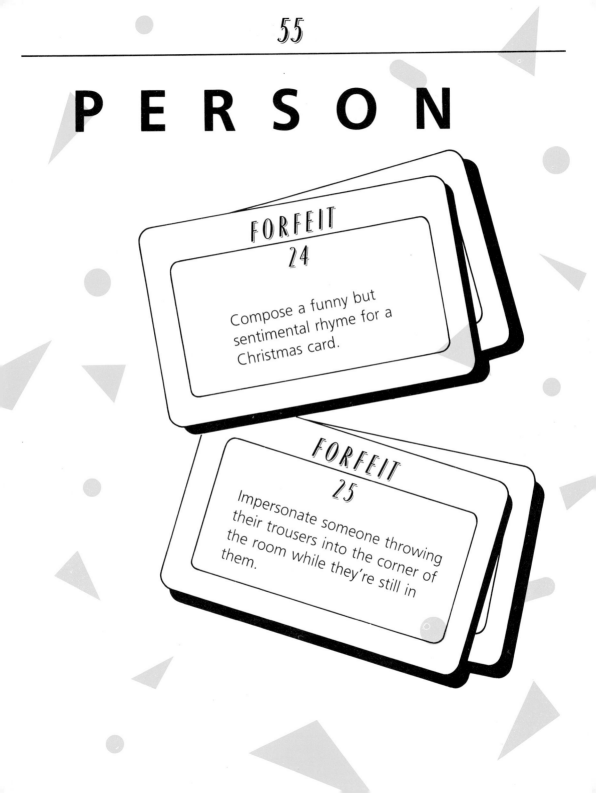

FORFEIT 24

Compose a funny but sentimental rhyme for a Christmas card.

FORFEIT 25

Impersonate someone throwing their trousers into the corner of the room while they're still in them.

TEAM SKIS

RULES

This game needs preparation. You need makeshift
skis formed by taking four planks about four feet long
by four inches wide. Nail three strips of material
across each plank at equal intervals to form
foot-straps.

Two teams of three put on these skis and agree a
race-track about twenty yards long.

If you cannot produce the skis, a similar effect can
be achieved by binding the legs together with rope.

HOW TO WIN

The first team to get every member around the race
track and over the finish line is the winner.

WHAT YOU NEED

Co-ordination and at least six players.

CHERNOBYL

RULES

In this game a group of players form a circle with arms linked to the player either side. In the middle of the circle a single player is enclosed, and it is their objective to escape from the enclosure by squeezing between legs or bodies. Meanwhile the circle tries to stop this happening.

WHAT YOU NEED

At least eight players.

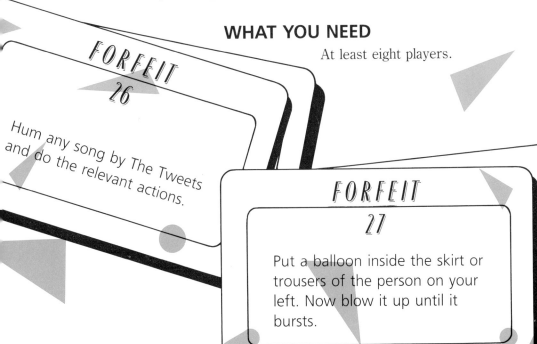

FORFEIT

26

Hum any song by The Tweets and do the relevant actions.

FORFEIT

27

Put a balloon inside the skirt or trousers of the person on your left. Now blow it up until it bursts.

JOURNEY GAMES

CHOPPER

RULES

One player thinks of an item and declares whether it is animal, vegetable or mineral. The others then take turns to guess what it is by asking up to twenty Yes/No questions about it.

HOW TO WIN

Avoid giving away what the item is in the twenty questions allowed.

WHAT YOU NEED

At least four players.

FORFEIT

28

Exchange three items of clothing with the person on your right.

Thesaurus

RULES

One player thinks of a word and everyone writes it down. Then all players must write down a set of words beginning with each letter from the nominated word, and with the same number of letters as the original nominated word.

When the results are produced points are only awarded for words which have not been used by anyone else.

HOW TO WIN

Get the most points.

RISKS

Good players risk becoming advertising executives.

FORFEIT
29

Balance a spoon on your nose for fifteen seconds.

Child

in the
Forest

RULES

Time for some psychology games. For this one you must tell your victims to imagine that they are in a dream, so they must let their imagination run free, and various adventures will happen to them. Firstly you say they are in a wood, so they must describe it. Then they are walking through the wood on a path, so they must describe that. Then they meet a bear in the wood which becomes increasingly aggressive so they must describe how they deal with it. Next they come to a river and finally to a house. In each case you must get them to describe as fully as possible what their feelings are during each encounter, what they do, and what the outcome is. Each player in the group should slowly build up their own story and then at the end you tell them what it all means.

Meaning: Each adventure represents some aspect of personality; the wood is your overall view of your life. The path is your path through life. The bear represents problems and how you face them. The river is sex and the house represents your view of your own death.

Sun Scoop

RULES

Each player has a sheet of paper and begins by writing an adjective, folding the paper over so that the writing is invisible, and passing it on for the next player to write a name drawn from the group of players.

The sequence continues with the paper being folded after each new word is added, until the folded papers include: adjective, name, verb, adjective, name, preposition, adjective, noun, followed by the word 'consequence' and a further adjective and noun. Eleven stages in total.

The sentences are then read out and the person mentioned in the most plausible circumstances along with the person mentioned most often must both do forfeits.

HOW TO WIN

Avoid being named.

WHAT YOU NEED

Pens and paper and at least five players.

Telegrams

RULES

One player is elected leader and he or she calls out twelve letters. The others write these letters down with a gap after each letter. They are then given two minutes to complete a telegram message with the twelve letters beginning each of the consecutive twelve words of the telegram.

HOW TO WIN

The most coherent or humorous telegram is the winner.

FORFEIT
30

Compose a limerick which includes the words of any *Sun* headline that you can remember.

PERES

RULES

One player begins by saying the first letter of a word. The next player must then add another letter with a specific word in mind. Letters can be added to the front or back, but they must always be part of a word while never forming a complete word.

If any player doubts that a sequence of letters could make up a word they may challenge, and whoever proves to be wrong is out.

HOW TO WIN

You must avoid completing a word and the game should be played repeatedly as a knock-out, so that the last one in is the winner.

WHAT YOU NEED

At least four players.

Λ>IOЯ

FORFEIT
31

Drink a dessertspoonful of tomato ketchup.

FORFEIT
32

Do the dance of the *Dying Swan*.

¿Enigma?

RULES

One player thinks of a word of six letters, then the others take turns in trying to find out what it is by volunteering a six-letter word of their own.

They can be told only how many times the letters in the volunteered word occur in the original word, and ultimately by comparing results the original word will become apparent.

HOW TO WIN

The first player to guess the real word is the winner.

WHAT YOU NEED

Pens and paper and at least four players.